Y0-AUX-324

Copyright©MCMLXXX by
The C.R.Gibson Company, Norwalk, Connecticut
All rights reserved
Printed in the United States of America
ISBN: 0-8378-3106-7

IF I ONLY HAD A HAMMER

A Do-It-Yourself Guide To Simple Home Maintenance

By Peter Seymour

The C.R.Gibson Company
Norwalk, Connecticut

Introduction

When the sink stops up and the dishwasher breaks down—and the ceiling is peeling and the window is stuck—and the shower keeps running but the vacuum won't—don't panic! And don't grab that phone; try checking this book. You'll find things to investigate *before* calling that expensive repair person. This handy volume is designed for all of you who don't think you can fix anything but wish you could. And you can!

Here is information about how things work inside, outside, all around the house—and hints on how to maintain them so they keep running better and longer. And when they *don't* work, there are tips on what to look for and easy-to-follow instructions for simple repairs and refurbishments.

You'll learn that many repairs and most household maintenance aren't as complicated as you think. You *can* learn to cure common ailments and you *can* learn to maintain the appliances, systems and structure of your home. And you'll save money in the process.

For more complicated repairs, we strongly advise you to call that master electrician, plumber or other highly skilled repair person. But you are going to be delighted with the ease with which many things around the house can be maintained, repaired and refurbished (especially if you can find the whatcha-ma-callit to adjust the whoo-sis on the thing-a-ma-bob!)

"The fellow
who owns a home
is always
just coming out
of a hardware store!"
     Kin Hubbard

Pay attention to the SIGHTS, SOUNDS and SMELLS of your home and the appliances in it. Your senses can tell you when a lot of things are beginning to wear out or are headed for trouble! You can repair or replace items before they cause real and costly trouble—a leaky pipe before it bursts, a smelly electric motor before it burns out, a refrigerator that runs and runs before it goes on the blink—because you didn't replace the door gasket. You can see when wood needs repainting, when the putty around a window should be replaced, when the sink is draining too slowly.
Be alert to symptoms!

7

HOME MAINTENANCE CHECK-UP RECOMMENDATIONS

At least once a year you should check the following and make repairs as needed:

Check window and door frames; replace rotted wood and worn-out weather-stripping.

Check pipes for leaks; pay particular attention to joints.

Repair broken ventilation screens or louvers (to prevent a squirrel or other critter from getting inside).

Clean gutters of leaves and other debris (check after storms, and especially in the autumn if you live where leaves fall). Also, be sure the runoffs at the bottom of downspouts are clear and properly carry off the water *away* from the foundation.

If you have a TV antenna, be sure it's securely fastened to the roof and properly grounded.

Check for loose nails or screws on hinges, siding, floors and door sills; anywhere you can think of! Pound in or tighten.

Check screens for needed repairs.

Check window panes to see if putty needs replacing.

Get up on the roof (very carefully—if you use a ladder, someone *must* hold it for you) and look for loose shingles or broken flashing. Also, cut away tree limbs that hang over the roof.

On driveways and walkways, repair holes and cracks.

Get your furnace serviced in the early fall. Replace filters (if your blower unit runs central air, too, replace filters spring and fall).

Look at electrical cords. Replace those that are frayed and worn. Also, look at the drop-lines that bring electrical power to your house; if they look frayed or worn, call your electric utility and ask them to come out and check.

Repaint exterior trim where it shows signs of weathering.

For Better Home Maintenance Keep

All guarantees and sales slips on items purchased, or for work done.

Manufacturers' instruction booklets.

Paint samples—in cans is best (dealers can match wet paint better than a dry chip).

Wallpaper samples, as well as samples of special flooring, ceramic tile, etc.

List of repair persons/contractors you've used or who have been specially recommended.

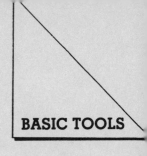

BASIC TOOLS

The usual complaint—and excuse—*for not doing a job right is: "I don't have the right tools!" I've discovered a lot of people try to repair things without proper tools. I used to, and sometimes still do! You've probably used a table knife instead of a screwdriver, a brick or a book instead of a hammer, tweezers instead of pliers, and even your teeth in place of scissors!*

Your chances for success go way down using such substitutes, while the probability goes way up that your temper will rise at an alarming rate!

There is an almost infinite assortment of tools—umpteen kinds and models and styles of hammers, wrenches, saws and so forth, not to mention all the specialized tools. Following are the most basic items, and a few variations, without which you shouldn't try to fix anything! Special tools will be mentioned as needed with specific repair jobs.

Tools are no more or less dangerous than most anything else you pick up: eating utensils, a sewing needle, a baseball bat, etc.

11

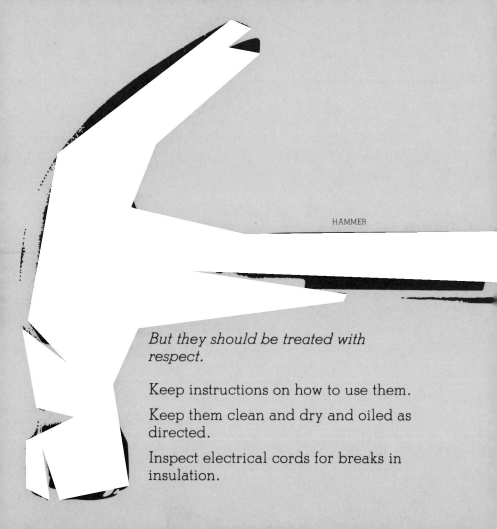

HAMMER

But they should be treated with respect.

Keep instructions on how to use them.

Keep them clean and dry and oiled as directed.

Inspect electrical cords for breaks in insulation.

Don't wear loose clothing or jewelry that might get caught in a tool. Be sure to wear the protective clothing that might be necessary for the job: hat, goggles, etc.

Keep tools sharp! A dull tool requires more effort and may cause more mistakes.

HAMMER: A 14 to 16 ounce *Curved Claw* hammer is recommended for pounding in (with the head) and taking out (with the claw) ordinary nails and tacks.

An *All-Steel* hammer is considered safest since the head can't fly off.

PLIERS: I've found two kinds of pliers are useful to have. The ordinary *Slip Joint* type 6″ size for gripping small nuts and other items...

PLIERS

and *Channel* or *Multiple Joint* type about 10″ long for larger objects.

Some people also like to have a *Long Nosed* plier for getting into very narrow small places.

CHANNEL PLIERS

LONG NOSED PLIERS

15

SCREWDRIVER

SCREWDRIVERS: You can avoid frustration if you have 3 different screwdrivers: small, medium and a *Phillips* head type.

Small: a 3/16" blade

Medium: a 5/16" blade

Phillips: a No. 2 blade (A Phillips head is for screws with a ⊕ head.)

You may want to buy the type of screwdriver that is reinforced by a metal shaft running completely through the handle.

The main problem with using a screwdriver seems to be that it seldom fits exactly into the screw head, it's too loose or hardly fits into the groove at all. So, you can buy an *all-purpose handle* with a set of various sized blades which may make life a little easier. Be sure to purchase a quality set!

In any case, use care when you insert or remove a screw *not* to ruin the groove in the head with a screwdriver that constantly slips out, bending and finally breaking the metal around the grooves.

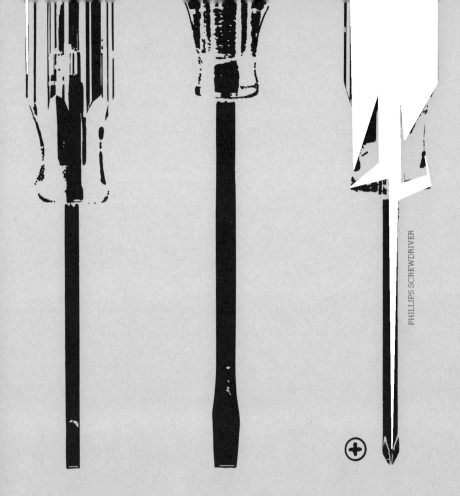

PHILLIPS SCREWDRIVER

17

WRENCH: One adjustable 10″ wrench
should be sufficient for small plumbing jobs
and items the pliers can't handle. Turn an
adjustable wrench clockwise to avoid
stripping the teeth on the adjusting part of
the wrench.

Not-so-basic wrenches that you may need
eventually:

A *Pipe Wrench* 18″ long, for larger
plumbing chores.

A set of *Open-Ended* Wrenches—various
sizes to fit various nut sizes.

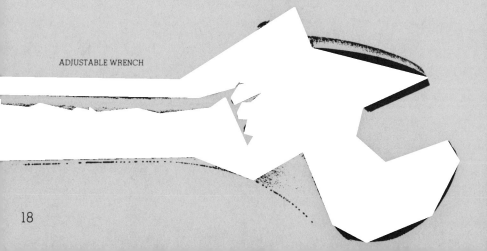

ADJUSTABLE WRENCH

PIPE WRENCH

OPEN-ENDED WRENCHES

19

A *Socket* Wrench set with a ratchet handle that lets you get into tight, crowded spaces, such as an automobile engine.

Finally, there are *Allen* Wrenches that look like this and are only used on items with hexagonal recessed heads (which you can't get at *without* an Allen Wrench!).

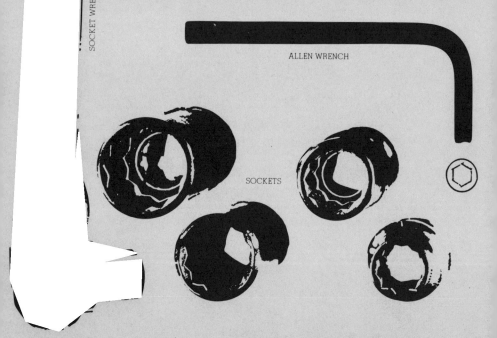

SOCKET WRENCH

ALLEN WRENCH

SOCKETS

MEASURING TOOLS: *A Tape Measure* (flexible steel that rolls back into its case) and a *Combination Square* (a 12″ ruler, plus adjustable right-angle side, with a built-in *level*) are both very useful, and beat the old yardstick and cloth measuring tape from the sewing box by a mile (or 1700 meters, at least)!

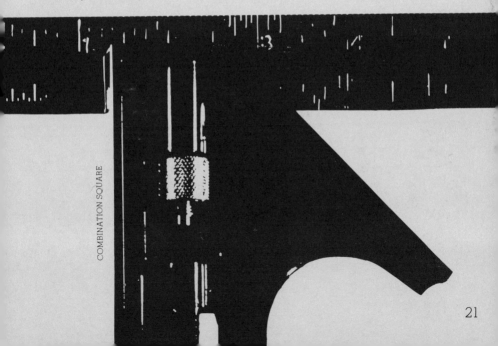

COMBINATION SQUARE

21

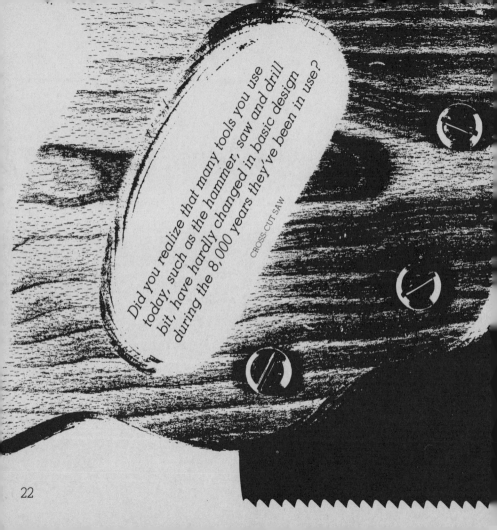

Did you realize that many tools you use today, such as the hammer, saw and drill bit, have hardly changed in basic design during the 8,000 years they've been in use?

CROSS-CUT SAW

22

SAW: An all-purpose *Cross-Cut* saw for cutting wood is a must—20 to 24 inches, with at least 8 teeth to the inch (the more teeth, the smoother the cut).

Buy a quality saw, and if you need it sharpened, have an expert do it.

Don't bang the teeth on anything...or try to saw through a nail!

The best way to *start a "cut"* is to draw the saw toward you first (starting the groove), then push the downstroke. You may need to do this several times before putting real pressure into the stroke.

HACK SAW

24

Sometimes a *Compass* or *Keyhole* saw comes in handy to make circular or straight cuts *inside* a board—to make an opening in a door or a wall, for example. Usually, you first *drill a hole* on the line you want to cut, then insert the saw.

If you need to cut *metal,* you'll need a *Hacksaw.* The best way to start a hacksaw cut is with a *file*—to establish the groove.

25

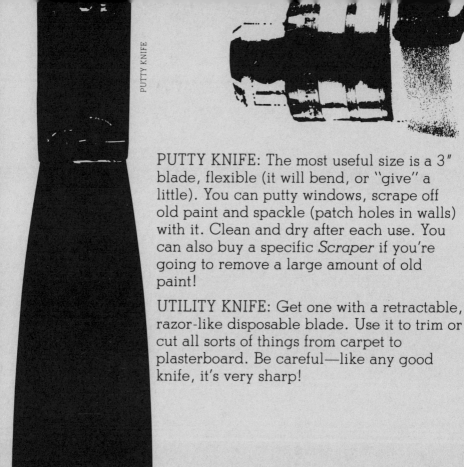

PUTTY KNIFE

PUTTY KNIFE: The most useful size is a 3″ blade, flexible (it will bend, or "give" a little). You can putty windows, scrape off old paint and spackle (patch holes in walls) with it. Clean and dry after each use. You can also buy a specific *Scraper* if you're going to remove a large amount of old paint!

UTILITY KNIFE: Get one with a retractable, razor-like disposable blade. Use it to trim or cut all sorts of things from carpet to plasterboard. Be careful—like any good knife, it's very sharp!

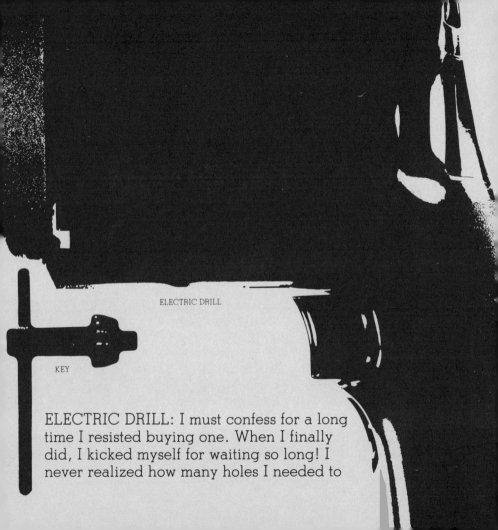

ELECTRIC DRILL

KEY

ELECTRIC DRILL: I must confess for a long
time I resisted buying one. When I finally
did, I kicked myself for waiting so long! I
never realized how many holes I needed to

drill, especially to make it easier to drive in screws.

Buy a 1/4" or 3/8" size drill—it will take various drill *Bits* up to that maximum size. You can get bits to drill through wood, metal and even masonry. They fit easily into the *Chuck* and are tightened with a *Key*.

Hint: Keep all your bits and the key in one place, a small box is a good idea, so you won't lose them.

Another Hint: Buy an extension cord for the drill; keep it with it, so you won't have to hunt one up when you need it. It's also a good idea to tape the key to the drill cord, about 18 inches from where the cord enters the drill handle. This way it is always handy.

When you drill a hole in wood for a screw, use a bit that's a little narrower than the screw threads, and don't drill the hole as deep as the screw should go in. That way there'll be wood left for the screw to latch onto.

28

Practice drilling holes in an old 2x4 to get the "feel" of the drill.

The neat thing about an electric drill (besides the feeling of power it gives you) is that in addition to drilling holes, it takes attachments that let you sand, buff, brush, mix and turn screws in and out. Ask at your hardware store for details.

Other Tools I've Found Handy

A toilet plunger.

Tin shears.

Scissors.

Clamps (to hold two pieces of wood together while glue dries, for example, or to hold wood steady while sawing it; you generally need a pair of clamps, at least, and should consult your hardware store for specific needs).

A medium duty punch.

A wood chisel.

A plane (for slicing off very thin bits of wood, such as when you have a door that sticks and need to remove a little from the top or bottom).

A nail set (to tap nails in *below* the wood surface).

Other Items to Keep on Hand

A quality pair of tight-fitting gloves (so you can feel what you're doing and still protect your hands).

A can of *light machine oil* to lubricate with and *penetrating oil* to help loosen screws and remove rust.

All purpose glue and an epoxy glue.

Some rope, heavy twine, wire, pencils.

Most of the nails, screws, nuts and bolts and
a thousand and one other items and
materials you might need can be purchased
when the need arises.

Thumbtacks.

Electrical tape and
masking tape.

PLANE

Hint: I suggest you keep an assortment of ordinary "box" nails of various lengths, however, as well as an assortment of nuts, bolts and washers (you can buy a small premixed assortment) and several sizes of wood screws.

Hint: Screws go in easier if you rub a little soap on the threads first.

To reuse an old screw hole that no longer holds a screw: put a piece of a wooden matchstick in the hole, or any small sliver of wood, and then insert screw.

It's generally accepted that the first man-made tools were fashioned 2 million years ago—crude, yes, but useful—made from stone and bone.

Sandpaper:
Sandpaper, more technically called "coated abrasives," comes marked from "Super Fine" to "Extra Coarse." You'll probably want "Medium" for general use preliminary sanding, and "Very Fine" for finishing jobs, but discuss your needs with the person at

the hardware store. "Coarse" is helpful in removing old paint.

The backing on sandpaper is usually paper; you can reinforce it with masking tape to keep it from tearing as you use it.

You can save money buying full sheets of sandpaper and cutting off small squares to use as you need them, rather than buying the precut packets or assortments.

Use sandpaper to sharpen your scissors, just cut a piece of sandpaper several times. Also, a SANDING BLOCK is useful and makes working with sandpaper easier.

Some 4,000 years ago, in the palace at Knossos on the island of Crete, there were · not only clay or terracotta "pipes" in use, but also a drainage system complete with toilet facilities.
This civilization was destroyed around 1400

B.C., and its "modern" plumbing system lost until archeologists discovered the ruins in this century.

The ancient Romans also devised a sanitary water supply and drainage system, with hundreds of public and private baths, fountains and water-flushed toilets. Some of the huge aqueducts built in the 3rd and 4th centuries A.D. to bring water into Rome are still standing and in use.

When barbarians overran Rome, however, the facilities were abandoned and the expertise lost. It was 1300 years before real plumbing systems emerged again in Europe—and reached America.

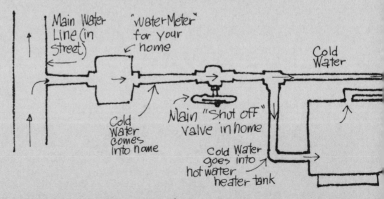

Main Water Line (in street)

"Water Meter" for your home

Cold Water

Cold Water comes into home

Main "Shut off" valve in home

Cold Water goes into hot water heater tank

*The simplest way to think of "Plumbing" is
to think of PIPES. Pipes that carry water. In
the old days, of course, there were no
pipes. You brought water up in a bucket,
out of a well. And sometimes the well went
dry!*

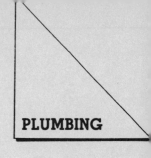

*All-in-all, pipes or plumbing have made
quite a difference in our daily lives.
Plumbing involves FAUCETS and VALVES,
too; and WATER PRESSURE and various
technical things. But we promised to keep
this simple! So, to show you in a simple way
how the concept of plumbing works in a
typical home, here's a simple diagram:*

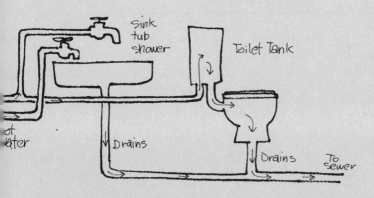

35

The Shut-Off Valve

First of all, and if you don't do anything else, locate the MAIN SHUT-OFF VALVE that turns off all the water into your home. Be sure you know where it is! If a pipe breaks or the water heater bursts, turn off the main shut-off valve—fast!

There are usually various "local" shut-off valves within your plumbing system. Locate these, also. For example, you'll find them on the pipes under a sink or the toilet tank.

Always, before starting to fix any part of your plumbing, turn off a "local" or the main shut-off valve.

Draining Your Plumbing System

It's easy!

1. Turn *off* main shut-off valve.
2. Turn *off* gas or electricity to hot water heater.
3. Turn *on* every faucet in your house, flush the toilets.
4. Wait 15-20 minutes.
5. Turn *off* all faucets and outlets.
6. Turn *on* main shut-off and gas or electricity.
7. Turn *on* all faucets and let them run until any sputtering and spritzing stops!

Plumbing Problems

The Big Drip

Most leaky faucets are usually caused by worn-out washers. There are various kinds of faucets, indoor and out, but they all work essentially the same way.

Here's how to change the washer on a leaky faucet:

Turn *off* water at local or main shut-off valve.

Turn *on* faucet you're going to fix, let leftover water run out. Turn off faucet.

Remove faucet *handle* and *stem* by unscrewing the "packing nut" with a wrench.

Lift out handle/stem.

On the bottom, a screw or nut holds a washer in place. Remove screw (nut) and washer.

Get a new washer just like it and fasten it

back in the bottom of the stem.

Replace handle/stem, tighten packing nut.

Turn *on* shut-off valve; turn on faucet. On some faucets the handle must be removed before you can get to the packing nut to remove the stem.

A packing nut often has a washer, too. You may need to replace this to stop water from seeping out around the nut.

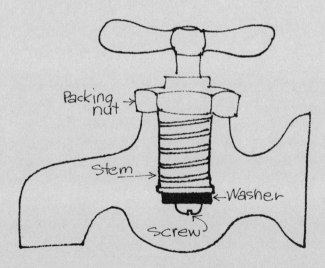

Slow-Running Faucet

First, keep faucet nozzles and shower heads *clean!* Water contains minerals that collect as sediment and can clog up the tiny openings in faucet and shower heads, often just enough to slow them down to an annoying dribble that speeds up your temper tantrum! Remove (usually unscrew) nozzle or head, soak overnight in all-purpose cleaner, scrub clean.

Don't waste time poking a pin into the little holes (a terribly temporary measure which I once tried).

The slow-water problem can also be caused by a build-up of material or an object stuck around the faucet stem. Remove stem and clean it. Also clean out around the pipe opening, reach in with a finger to be sure nothing's blocking the water flow (I once found an old washer which had somehow fallen in and gotten scrunched around to block most of the water flow). If you still aren't getting enough water, the cause is

probably a corroded pipe somewhere...
call a plumber or put up with the dribble.

Leaky Pipe

Often caused by old age or corrosion.
Before replacing a leaky pipe, or a section
of it, or a leaky joint (where 2 or more pipes
are joined) try the following:

Buy a RUBBER PATCH and METAL CLAMP
SET at the hardware store. Be sure it's the
right size for the pipe. It goes on easily,
using a screwdriver. This may last a long
time...or only temporarily.

Use some epoxy cement, especially if
pressure isn't high and leak is small. Turn
off water first and *dry* leak area before
applying cement. This can work well
around *joints.* However, it's usually a
temporary repair.

At a leaky joint, try just *tightening* it with a
wrench! I've personally stopped a slow leak
in various old pipes by wrapping the leak

tightly with a strip of cloth and sealing it with friction tape.

I've also heard of people using a wad of chewing gum, held in place with tape!

For small leaks, push a pencil point into the hole and snap it off. Then tape the area with heavy tape.

In cold climates. . .pipes can freeze! Frozen water expands, and can burst a pipe. When the water thaws, you'll have a small flood! You don't have to worry about pipes freezing in most modern houses. . .unless a storm or some other event causes your heating system to be off for a day or more and the temperature is below freezing for an extended period.

Under these conditions (which happened to me in the midwest after an ice storm) it's wise to drain the water out of your plumbing system (see "Draining Your Plumbing System"). You'll be without water until the heat returns or the temperature rises, but you'll protect your system from the possibility of very costly repairs.

REMEMBER:
Shut off and drain *outside* pipes before the first freeze of winter.

Interesting Note: Hot water pipes seem to freeze before cold water ones!

The Water Hammer

Do your pipes sometimes make a racket like they're trying to play the "Anvil Chorus"? It's annoying, but not serious.
You see, when you turn off a faucet, all that water gushing out is suddenly stopped. There has to be some leeway in the pipes for the water to back up or overflow into, or else it will make the pipes vibrate and "hammer" for a few moments.
Most systems have "air chambers" that absorb the "shock" of the water pressure each time you turn off a faucet. Over the years, these "air cushions" can leak away, and your pipes start to hammer and yammer. To fix the situation, simply drain your plumbing system. (See page 37.)

Unstopping Drains

A clogged drain can be anything from a nuisance to a disaster! It's usually an expensive plumber's call, but remember it *is* a job you can do yourself in many cases!

First, some *Preventive Medicine:*

Don't put anything but waste water down sink drains!

Keep grease and coffee grounds and garbage out of the kitchen sink (obviously you can forget the warning on garbage if you have a garbage disposal unit).

Strange as it seems . . . there are some 300 feet of water and drain pipes in the average house, enough to run the length of a football field.

Keep hair and lint out of bathroom sinks.

Don't flush unflushables down the toilet.

Pour a little chemical drain cleaner down each drain from time to time. BUT REMEMBER: A CHEMICAL DRAIN CLEANER IS POISON; IT CAN BURN YOUR SKIN OR EAT INTO YOUR CLOTHING. DON'T BREATHE THE FUMES.

Check your stack vent(s)—this is the vent that sticks up above the roof, connected to an *empty* pipe that allows gases to escape from the plumbing system; be sure the vent isn't clogged with leaves or other debris, or in winter frozen over with ice or snow.

No matter how careful you are, drains will get clogged. If *all* drains in your home become clogged or sluggish, your main drain is messed up...and you'd better call a plumber. Sorry!

Unclogging a Sink Drain

Use a *Rubber Plunger,* the old "Plumber's Helper." If there's a "pop-up" drain plug, or stopper, in the drain, remove it. You can usually do this by turning it and pulling it out. In some cases, you may have to unscrew the assembly under the sink so you can pull out the rod that holds and works the plug. Clean off the plug.

Stuff a rag into the sink overflow opening.

Put a little petroleum jelly on the rubber rim of the plunger cup for better "sealing."

Be sure water covers the plunger when it's over the drain opening.

Pump plunger up and down—a smooth downstroke and a "jerk" upstroke. If drain doesn't open up in a minute or so, you'll need to try something else.

You can try a *Chemical Drain Cleaner.* I have personally found chemical cleaners to work temporarily. CAREFULLY FOLLOW DIRECTIONS ON CONTAINER.

Don't use if the drain is totally stopped, if there's no movement of water at all.

Never use a rubber plunger after you've put chemical cleaner into the drain.

If you plan to try the next method— "Cleaning out the TRAP"—do not use a chemical cleaner!

Cleaning The Trap

The TRAP is the U-shaped piece of pipe under the sink. Put a bucket under this to catch leftover water.

If there's a CLEAN-OUT PLUG in the trap, then unscrew and remove it. A lot of the clogging "yuck" may come out this opening. Poke around with a piece of stiff wire. Run water into the sink to help flush stoppage out the open plug hole into the bucket.

If there's no clean-out plug, remove the trap. Just unscrew (counterclockwise) the SLIP NUTS. Each should have a RUBBER WASHER (gasket); when replacing the trap, install new washers if the old ones look worn.

Clean out the trap and pipes it attaches to.

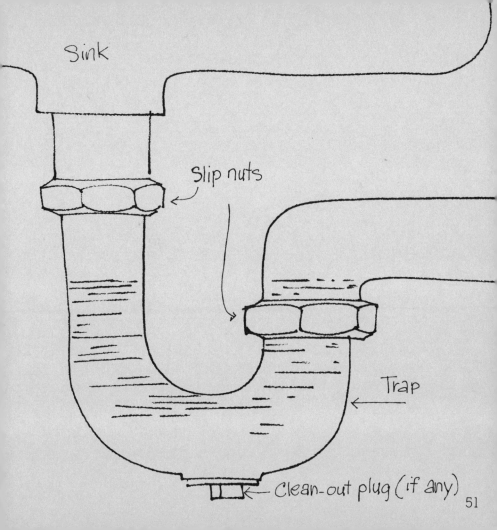

Sink

Slip nuts

Trap

Clean-out plug (if any)

51

The Drain Auger or "Snake"

Owning one could save you a plumber's call. Hardware stores generally have them at moderate cost.

Push the SNAKE through the clean-out plug, or after removing trap, directly into the pipe.

When AUGER or snake seems to stop, don't force it. Pull it out a bit, then start again. Work it back and forth.

In 1851 when the White House announced that a bathroom was going to be installed, a number of irate citizens put up quite a hue and cry against such a needless expense!

For Tub or Shower Drains

You generally can't get to the trap, it's behind the wall or beneath the floor.

A snake is your best bet, although you can also try the plunger first. With the snake, go through the overflow tube opening, if possible (or through the drain opening itself). Remember—if there's a pop-up drain stopper, remove it first.

Toilet Drain

The usual toilet drain has a trap behind it, inside the seat. If an unflushable item gets flushed, it will probably only go as far as the trap and clog things up there. Try a Plumber's Helper! If that *doesn't* help... Call the plumber...or get very brave and try the following.

If toilet is full, bail out excess water with a pan into a bucket.

Wear a rubber glove. Reach down into bowl, back and up into trap area. If anything *is* stuck there, you'll probably feel it and can pull it out.

A special toilet auger is available, but that begins to get more complicated.

The Touchy Toilet Tank

The toilet tank mechanism is quite simple, but sometimes quite touchy. A gentle tightening here, a little attention there, will often work wonders!

First—see how it works: When you press down the FLUSH HANDLE, the TANK BALL is lifted from the FLUSH VALVE allowing water *out* of the tank. The FLOAT falls as the water goes out, and this *opens* the BALL-COCK (or INTAKE VALVE), allowing water to *refill* the tank. As the water rises, so does the Float. When water, and float, reach the appropriate level, this shuts *off* the Ball-Cock.

Before attempting most tank repairs, turn off

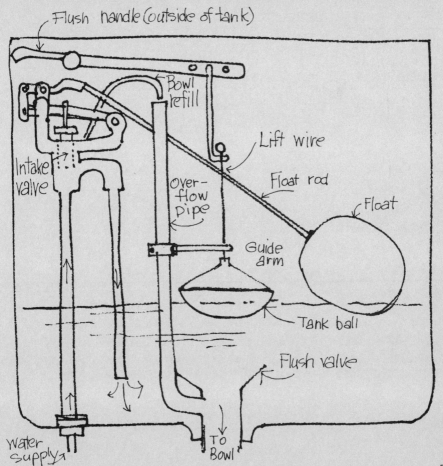

Flush handle (outside of tank)

Bowl refill

Lift wire

Float rod

Float

Intake valve

Over-flow pipe

Guide arm

Tank ball

Flush valve

Water supply

To Bowl

55

the water coming into the tank. Then flush. Now you have an empty tank!

Here are two common toilet tank problems...and what you might be able to do about them.

Problem One: Water runs, but tank won't fill up *or* water keeps running even though tank seems to be full!

The Tank Ball may be worn out and not seating correctly on the Flush Valve, so that water leaks out around it, into the bowl. *Replace the Ball.* It generally just screws off the end of the LIFT WIRE.

The Lift Wire, on the end which screws the Tank Ball, may be bent or crooked so that it doesn't lead the Ball down directly over the Flush Valve. Carefully watch its action after flushing, and *adjust it,* if possible, as necessary.

The Flush Valve itself may get gummy with sediment so that the Ball won't seat tightly. *Clean Valve* with steel wool.

The Float may be worn out and need to be replaced. It screws onto the end of the Float Rod.

The Float Rod may need to be *bent downwards* a little. Hold rod in both hands and bend slightly in middle.

The Ball-Cock is leaking! The washer or entire valve may need replacing.

Problem Two: The toilet won't flush properly.

There may not be a full tank of water because the Float Rod is bent *too far* down, causing the Float to shut off the Ball-Cock (Intake) Valve too soon. Try bending the rod *up* a little.

The Tank Ball may seat *too soon,* before enough water has left the tank to complete the flush. Either put on a new Ball...or raise the Guide Arm; it's usually attached by a screw to the Overflow Pipe and can be moved up or down the pipe.

After any work on the tank, be sure the Refill Tube is stuck in the Overflow Pipe.

Cracks Around Tub or Shower

The filler that goes between tub or shower and the wall to keep water from getting down into the wall will wear out eventually or break in places. It's easily replaced with PLASTIC SEALER that comes in a tube; available at hardware stores.

First, remove the old filler and clean the surface. Be sure it's dry before applying the sealer.

Squeeze sealer into the opening. Smooth with a putty knife.

Caution: Work fast! The sealer dries in minutes. You can, instead, install *Crescent-Shaped Tiles around the tub rim, next to the wall, to keep water out. This is a longer-lasting sealing method, but takes more time and effort.*

You install the tiles in *mastic.* Most paint, hardware or building supply stores that sell you the materials will tell you how.

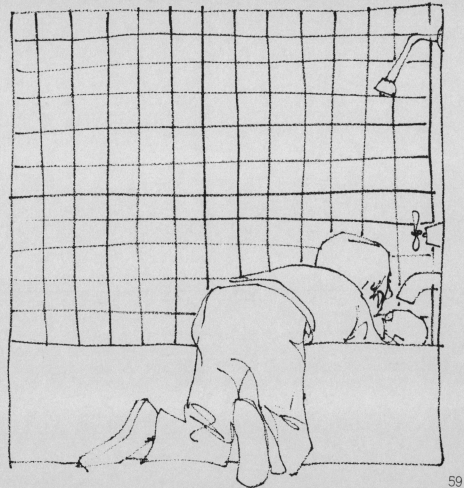

59

The Hot Water Heater

If you note a leak in your hot water heater
tank, replace the tank at once—before it
bursts! There's no way to repair a leaky
tank.

Be sure your water heater tank is *level*.

A temperature setting of 140 to 160 degrees
should be adequate. This will save energy
and increase the life of the tank.

Every couple of months, drain off the
sediment from the tank, there's a drain
faucet at the base of the tank.

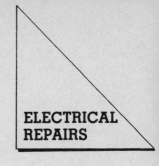

It is not within the scope or purpose of this book to provide you with anything but the simplest information about the electrical system in your home, or about how to fix things electric. My advice is "Call an electrician." Unfortunately, these days you may have to wait a week for one to arrive, but that beats short-circuiting your blood vessels!

ELECTRICAL REPAIRS

Some Basics

Know where your CIRCUIT BREAKER or FUSE BOX is located. Know where the main

power switch is, also, to turn off all electricity for the whole home.

Find out which lights, switches and outlets each fuse or circuit breaker controls. When you flip a circuit breaker off or remove a fuse, there is no electricity, or current, flowing to the outlets or switches controlled by it.

If there is an electrical "overload" caused by a malfunction of an appliance or too many "amps" on the wires, the circuit breaker will automatically "break" the circuit (flip to off) or the fuse will "blow" (burn out) to avoid burning up the wire and causing a fire.

Fuses: Never replace a fuse with a higher *amp* than called for. Don't put a 25 amp fuse in a 20 amp spot. The amp requirements are normally listed on the fuse box.

When changing fuses, don't stand in water or touch a water or gas pipe. You can get an insulated FUSE REMOVER at most hardware stores. Keep an extra supply of fuses in the proper amp ratings.

Keep a flashlight handy to check fuse box or circuit breakers.

When an electrical appliance, light or outlet doesn't work, check to be sure the fuse isn't blown or circuit breaker flipped to "off" before worrying about repairs. Of course, in the case of lights, be sure the *bulb* hasn't burned out. . .or the cord is not unplugged.

Any bare spots in an electrical cord or wire (the insulation or covering material frayed or broken) should be repaired or replaced at once. BE SURE IT IS UNPLUGGED OR THE CURRENT IS OFF BEFORE WORKING ON A WIRE.

Never buy any electrical appliance or equipment or materials without a UL label *(Underwriters Laboratories).*

What is a kilowatt? Your utility bill probably measures your electrical usage in terms of Kilowatt Hours. A kilowatt equals 1000 Watts. A 100 watt bulb burning for 10 hours equals 1000 watts (100 times 10) or one Kilowatt Hour.

For reference: A radio uses about 40 watts per hour.

To keep an extension cord from pulling out of the appliance or tool it's connected to, loop the two cords together before plugging them in.

Extension Cord

Appliance Cord

Repairing an Electric Plug

A cracked or broken electric plug should
be replaced at once. Sometimes they get
stepped on or otherwise smashed.
Sometimes the wire leading into the plug
gets cracked and frayed, which is just as
bad. So, you are either replacing the wire
or the plug. *Attaching* new wire to old plug,
or new plug to old wire, is what this is all
about, in any case! If the wire is regular
lamp cord and will carry no more than 300
watts (use no larger than a 300 watt bulb),
you can use a "snap on" plug. You can get
one at any hardware store and at many
supermarkets.
On the back is a small "lever" that opens so
that the wire can be inserted. Split the wire
about ¼ " before inserting. Push wire in,
snap lever closed. That's it!

If you use an old or standard plug, or a heavy-duty one to carry higher wattage, you'll have to screw the two wires onto their terminals: Push the cord through the plug.

Separate cord into its 2 wires and peel off the insulation about ½ " with a small knife. Be careful not to cut the wire fibers. You can buy a "wire stripper" gadget that cuts the insulation but not the wire!

Twist the fibers on each wire, clockwise.

Pull one wire around each terminal, and then wrap it around a screw, clockwise.

Tighten screws to hold wire.

Insulation should come up to screw, but not be under it.

Put cover back over plug.

Put a New On-Off Switch on a Lamp

For standard, screw-in bulb type lamps, unplug lamp.

Remove shade and bulb.

Now . . . notice the outer covering of the socket—the metal piece with the switch, that the bulb screwed into: if it hasn't worn off (you should have such an old lamp!) the word "press" will be visible. Take hold of the covering, thumb on the word "press"— and press and gently pry the covering off.

Next slide off the inner "insulator" sleeve. Pull the switch out of the socket base so you can get at the two wires and screws.

Unscrew and detach wires. Get a new switch that fits the lamp. Reattach wires to screws on new switch. Always wrap wires clockwise around screw; when the screw is tightened, the wire is drawn in and tightened.

Slide everything together again!

Never pull a plug out of a socket by the cord, always hold onto the plug.

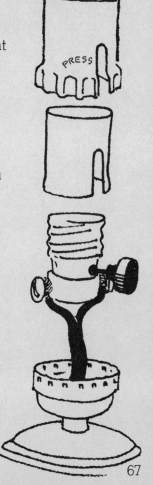

Keep electrical cords away from heat, which can dry them out and cause them to crack. Also, keep cords from under rugs, as they may become worn and frayed and can cause a fire.

EXTENSION CORDS: Regular line cord is okay for lamps and small appliances. Use *heavy duty* extension cords rated for power tools.

An OUTDOOR EXTENSION CORD should be the 3-wire variety, the third wire is for grounding. Ask at the hardware store where you buy the cord how to ground it properly for your circumstances.

Most experts agree that you should not have more than one appliance plugged into an extension cord—or at least don't have more than one *going* at once.

If you buy a power tool such as a drill, with a 3-pronged plug, get an ADAPTER that converts it to 2-prongs for insertion in most normal outlets.

When there is a power failure (all the electricity in the house goes off), *unplug* or be sure to *turn off* refrigerator, air conditioner and TV set so that a sudden surge of power, when it's restored, won't damage the motor or circuitry.

Basic Hint: Whenever you take something apart, notice very carefully the order in which the pieces come off; then you will have less of a problem putting them back together properly. It also helps to lay out the parts in the sequence they are removed, *as they are being removed.* You may want to label the parts or draw yourself a simple diagram. This can be very useful if you will not be reassembling the object immediately.

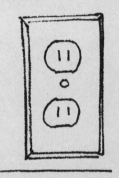

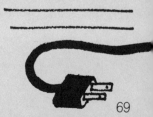

Ever notice some unexplained or sudden *static* in your radio or TV? Was one of your electric appliances on at the time—vacuum, mixer, can opener, etc.? If so, the static is a warning that the appliance should be checked for possible worn wiring or parts.

Whenever an electric appliance doesn't work, check to be sure the outlet it's plugged into is carrying "juice" by plugging in something, such as a lamp you know is working.

Caution: Anytime you turn on an electric appliance or motor, and it blows a fuse or circuit breaker, DO NOT USE THE APPLIANCE AGAIN UNTIL IT IS CHECKED AND REPAIRED.

Hanging Things on Walls

A key element to know about is locating STUDS! Why? Well, perhaps you've experienced the mess of hanging something heavy—traverse rods for drapes, bookshelves or large mirrors, for example— and having them fall down because you fastened them in just the wallboard or plaster...and not in the wooden studs (the 2x4s) spaced vertically every so often behind the walls.

The every so often is actually every 16 inches, or should be (some cheaper construction has 'em every 24 inches).

INSIDE YOUR HOUSE OR APARTMENT

To Find the Studs

I'm told you can buy a "magnetic" stud-finder that is attracted to the nails inside the wall, in the studs. I usually try the "knock" method: rap on the wall—there's a more solid sound over a stud, a hollower sound where one isn't. You can also measure from one corner, every 16 inches (plus the 1½ inch width of the stud) should get you a stud. No method, it seems, is infallible! The only way to be *sure* there's a stud is to drill a hole in the wall a few inches above the floor, so you can patch it easily and obscurely. Once you do locate a stud, there probably is one 16-18 inches on either side (allowing for its width).

Wall Fasteners

There is a vast variety of items for securing things to walls. Here are a few:

Screws, of course, are fine for fastening all sorts of things to wood (frames, studs or thick paneling).

Adhesive fasteners work for lightweight items on glass, wallboard and smooth plaster. They are not very good on wood, and personally, I've found they can dry out and fall off wherever they're stuck.

Picture hooks are okay for lightweight items on wallboard, plaster and wood. On plaster, I like to put a little piece of tape on the wall to keep the nail from cracking the plaster.

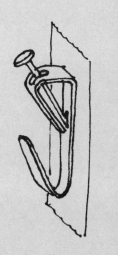

Anchor-type fasteners are the most reliable and easiest to use for normal jobs. There are various kinds for various substances (seldom for wood, however). They go into the wall, and then open up or expand to a certain extent to hold firm. They seem to be essential for ceramic tile, stucco, brick, etc. Lead-type anchors are recommended fasteners for masonry, stucco and brick.

Toggle bolts are anchor-type fasteners that can be used for wood, plaster and gypsum board.

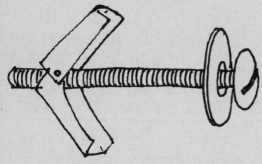

Putting On a Curtain Rod...Straight

One way to get a rod up straight is simply to measure both sides (and the middle for a center bracket) from the same part of the window, usually the top of the frame. I've also used the following technique.

Cut a piece of cardboard into this shape (6 or 8 inches long). Fit it above one top corner of the window. Mark the holes where you'll screw in the bracket. Now "flip" the cardboard to the other side. The holes should be in the same relative position for that bracket. Of course, sometimes the window frame has gotten crooked!

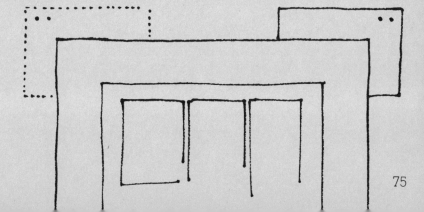

75

To Fix Scratched Wood Paneling

Ever hear of COLORED PUTTY PENCILS?
Get one that matches the color of your wood
paneling, color in the scratch! Putty pencils
are also great to touch up any nail heads
that are showing.

For larger scratches or even small gouges
in paneling, use *wood putty.* Stain it to
match the wood as closely as possible.

Wood paneling can be waxed, by the way,
to help protect it as you would fine
furniture.

To Protect Against Pipe Freeze-Up

If you have exposed pipes, in crawl spaces or other areas where there's no heat, wrap the pipes in insulation.

In very cold weather, let the faucet *drip* to keep water running slightly in the pipe; this can often prevent a total freeze-up.

If you plan to be away from your house and plan to leave it unheated for part of the winter, drain the plumbing system.

A pipe is probably frozen when no water comes out of the faucet, and it's cold winter weather. Find the frozen portion by following the pipe to its exposed area and *feeling* it.

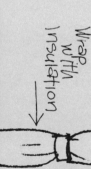

Wrap
w/th
Insulation

To Thaw a Frozen Pipe

Leave faucet open (on) and try a hair dryer, heat lamp or electric heating pad or blanket; if you have none of these, even a high-watt light bulb held near the pipe may work.

DO NOT TOUCH THE PIPE ITSELF WHILE OPERATING AN ELECTRICAL ITEM. Wrap the pipe first if you are using an electric blanket or pad, then plug it in. After use, unplug and then unwrap.

Try *hot* towels held against the pipe, change 'em often. At many hardware stores you can buy "heating tape" that plugs into a regular socket, instructions come with it.

Spackling

You can fix scratches, cracks and small holes and other bumps and bruises in plaster and wallboard walls with some fine sandpaper, SPACKLING COMPOUND and a putty knife. You can buy premixed spackling compound or the dry powder (cheaper) and mix it with water yourself.

Clean away loose debris from crack or hole. Apply the spackling compound. Smooth out with putty knife, wipe away excess. When good and dry, sandpaper it smooth. Touch up with matching paint.

Hint: Large areas or deep gouges may require more than one coating. Apply the spackle in layers rather than one heavy application. Always let the area dry and sand it before repeating applications.

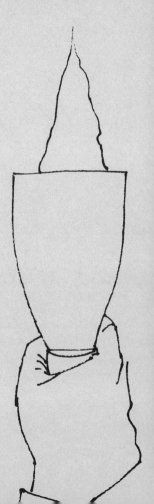

Sticky Windows and Drawers

Rub the track with soap or paraffin...or buy a special silicone lubricant for the purpose. Sometimes a drawer needs to be *sanded* to make it slide easily (often because the wood has swollen). To find out where it needs sanding, mark the tracks with a crayon, slide drawer in and out as best you can, then see where the crayon has rubbed off on the drawer.

Opening Painted-Shut Windows

I've inherited a few of these, and in the old days I probably left a few for others to cope with! What an aggravating and back-wrenching affair! To open, try this: with a sharp knife cut around the whole sash next to the frame, cutting through the paint. Next, wedge a chisel or screwdriver between window sash and sill along various places (tap in with a hammer) and try to pry window up. Be careful not to dent the wood as you pry. You may have to tap around the whole window sash with a hammer (wrap it in a washrag so you don't harm the wood) to break the window free from the paint.

How To Putty a Window

With a little patience, anyone can learn to do this! Putty is fun stuff, too, kind of like modeling clay. It comes in cans and is really called "glazing compound." Be sure to keep the lid on tight or it'll dry up.

Let's say you have a cracked or broken window pane. Here's how to replace it.

First, remove the broken pane. Wear heavy gloves. Some people like to knock out the pane (being careful not to scatter glass all over the place) and then remove the old putty with a chisel or putty knife.

Other people put masking tape (or even a square of contact paper) over the glass to keep it from breaking further, then remove the old putty and take the pane out in several (or even one) pieces.

Also, remove the GLAZIER'S POINTS, the little metal triangles.

Second, measure the *inside* dimensions of the opening. The hardware store or glass company will either have a standard pane or cut one to fit (usually taking 1/8th inch off the measurement to allow for expansion of the wood frame).

With the new pane at hand, now coat the frame into which it will fit with *linseed oil*, if possible, to keep the new putty from drying too fast.

Next, put a light layer of putty around the frame, not very much at all. Put the new pane in place, pushing into the layer of putty.

Secure it with glazier's points, two per side. You can try to push them into the same places they were before. Or tap them in with hammer and flat side of screwdriver blade. Don't hit the glass!

Now, roll a nice ball of putty in your palms, then roll it out into a long "snake" or *bead* and press it around the glass along the frame with your fingers. Smooth it out at an angle with a putty knife to resemble the other puttied panes in the window. Wait three days for putty to dry before painting.

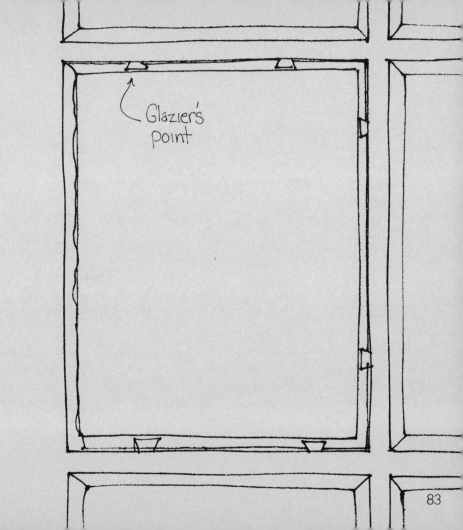

Glazier's
point

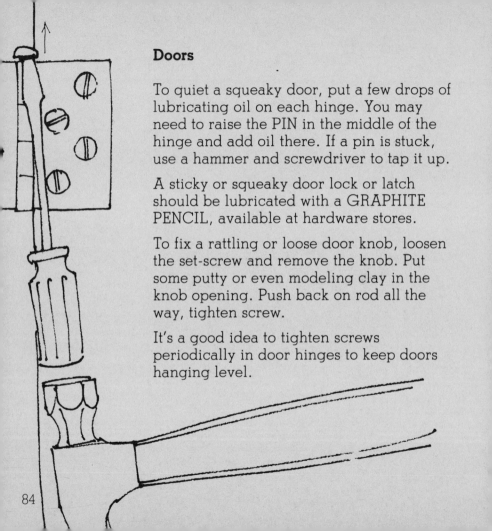

Doors

To quiet a squeaky door, put a few drops of lubricating oil on each hinge. You may need to raise the PIN in the middle of the hinge and add oil there. If a pin is stuck, use a hammer and screwdriver to tap it up.

A sticky or squeaky door lock or latch should be lubricated with a GRAPHITE PENCIL, available at hardware stores.

To fix a rattling or loose door knob, loosen the set-screw and remove the knob. Put some putty or even modeling clay in the knob opening. Push back on rod all the way, tighten screw.

It's a good idea to tighten screws periodically in door hinges to keep doors hanging level.

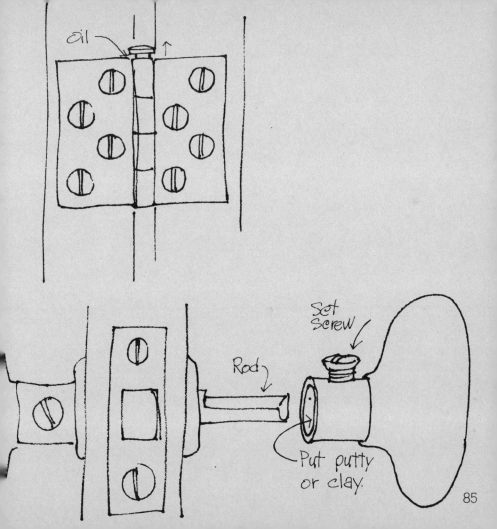

oil

Set
Screw

Rod

Put putty
or clay.

85

Make Wooden Coat Hooks...or Hooks for
Various Light-Load Purposes.

Get some DOWELLING (usually these
round "pins" come in 3-foot lengths). Saw
into desired hook lengths, perhaps
3 inches. Get some 2" finishing nails. Drill
a hole in the dowel about 1" in depth, using
a bit size just big enough so the nail will fit
in the hole. Hammer nails in where you
want the hooks, leaving about an inch of the
nail exposed. Stick the dowel on the nail.

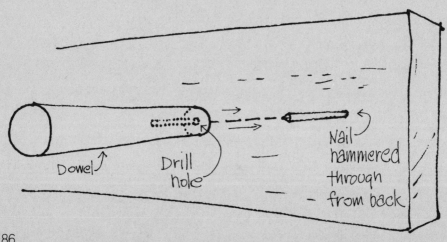

Dowel

Drill
hole

Nail
hammered
through
from back

Laying Floor Tiles

You can easily lay new tiles in kitchen or bathroom or elsewhere by following directions on the box they come in, and asking about it where you buy the tiles. Be sure you carefully measure the space to be tiled. Here are a few hints.

Work from the *center* out (don't start at one wall).

To find the center of the room, measure the center of opposite walls, at the floor attach a *chalk line* to tacks at these center points and snap it to mark a straight line across the floor.

Note: You can buy ready-made *chalk line* (like string marked with chalk). You stretch it tightly across the area to be marked, then lift it leaving an easy-to-follow straight line.

Now, measure the center of the chalk line,

and you have the center of the room (or floor). Using a square, along the chalk line at the center point, mark a line perpendicular to the chalk line. Start your first tile exactly at the angle made by the 2 lines. Go from there! You can cut tiles to fit along the wall, where they're hardly noticeable.

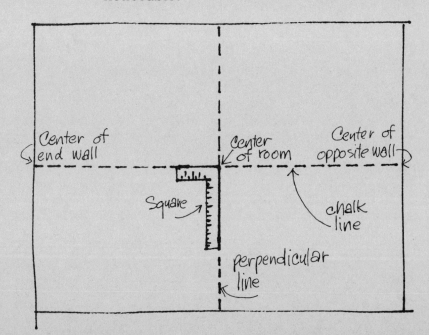

Wallpapering

Wallpapering is best left to experts, but if you're adventurous you may want to try it yourself. Good luck! I admit I hate to wallpaper! (Nowadays "wallcovering" is more accurate since besides paper, you can get vinyls and fabrics, foiled and flocked and embossed in all sorts of designs.) The following suggestions and hints work for other people, but I'm all thumbs.

First of all, wallpapering takes *planning*. You must carefully measure the space to be covered, and take into account any *pattern* matching that's necessary.

I'm told a single roll of wallpaper covers 35 square feet, no matter how wide it is. After trimming, you can figure on covering more like 30 square feet. Wallpaper comes in various *widths*, most usually 18 or 30 inches wide.

Be sure the wall is clean...and all holes have been patched.

If you are papering over *old paper*...
remove any torn or loose pieces. (Any old
paper which is still clinging to the wall
should be feathered with sandpaper.)
Sometimes this can get to be a real mess! If
you have to remove a lot of paper, consider
renting a wallpaper STEAMER or try a
chemical remover.

If you have a long table available, use it.
Otherwise, use the floor to roll out, measure
and cut wallpaper strips, and to apply the
paste. Cover table or floor with newspapers
or drop cloth to protect against the mess
you'll probably create!

Cut to length all the strips you'll need and
stack them up. Always *add* about 6 inches
to the length (3 at top, 3 at bottom) which
will give you some leeway in adjusting the
strips for pattern matches...and also
ensures that you don't cut a strip too short!

Trim off top and bottom after strip is on the
wall. Use a RAZOR KNIFE if the trim line is
smooth; if not, mark the line, peel back
paper and cut with scissors.

If you can find a pattern you like in *prepasted* paper, use it and avoid having to mix and apply the paste!

Actually, the paste isn't that hard to mix. Follow directions on box or bag. One pound (of wheat paste) will take care of 6 or 7 rolls. You need special adhesives with various kinds of wallcoverings, ask where you buy your material. There's a mildew resistant adhesive recommended for a coated wallcovering.

Apply paste with a PASTE BRUSH. Use plenty of it, especially along the edges. Let it set up a minute or so before hanging. You can fold the paper ⅓ way back on itself (sticky side) to make it easier to pick up and handle.

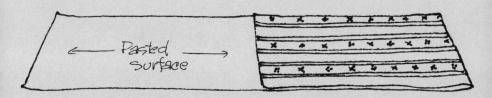

← Pasted → Surface

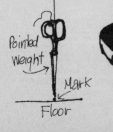

Tack at ceiling

String

Pointed Weight

Mark

Floor

Be sure the first strip goes up *straight*! Use a "plumb line" to establish an accurate line.

Note: A PLUMB LINE is a weight (bob) on the end of a string...the weight or bob ought to have a pointed end, use a heavy nail or scissors.

Tack string to molding around ceiling, or at top of wall...then mark where the bob points along the bottom of the wall.

Snap a chalk line (see "Laying Floor Tiles") to mark the straight line.

Place the paper on the wall first at the *top*. You can slide it into exact position, aligning it with the chalk line.

Use a SMOOTHING BRUSH to smooth out the paper and get rid of any air bubbles. Work from the center out.

Now, unfold the bottom ⅓ of the strip and smooth it into place.

When you put the *second* strip up, slide it carefully seam to seam with the first. You can buy a SEAM ROLLER to roll the adjoining seams flat.

Use a damp sponge to remove excess paste from seams or edges or from the pattern side.

Normally, you do not put a seam in the corner of a room. Go a couple of inches "around the corner."

Because walls often don't join very straight, you should make a plumb line around each corner (if you want everything perfectly shipshape) and trim the length of paper to keep it straight. This may cause a pattern match to go slightly off...but that's better than crooked paper...I think!

If the wall you're papering has a window or door, start papering from it and move toward where walls join.

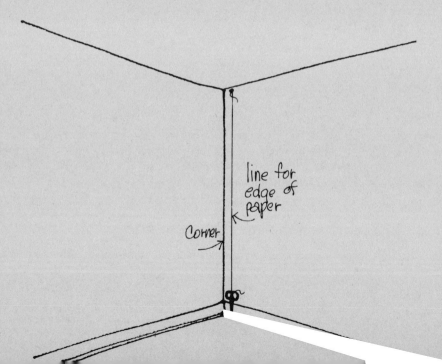

line for edge of paper

Corner

On new plaster, or over glossy paint, apply a coat of *sizing* before papering.

Save all excess paper to use to patch small areas around frames and in corners.

Don't buy inexpensive lightweight paper! It makes the job much harder. A quality, medium weight makes the most sense.

If a "bubble" later develops in your wallpaper, try this: With a razor cut a small X in the bubble, lift the flaps this creates, put a bit of glue on them, smooth down. Or. . .just leave the bubble alone!

Vinyl-coated wall coverings are a good idea if you have young children. You can wipe off handprints and other "greasies" with a damp cloth or sponge.

Remember: You can get matching drapery material to go with certain wallpaper patterns!

On Prepasted Paper: You need to buy a "water box" to fit the width of the paper, or if you have a tub that's wide enough, use that. You soak the paper in water for about a minute (or whatever the manufacturer says) before hanging (reroll the strip glue-side out before putting it into the water). Don't wet the glue side with brush or sponge; you could remove most of the sticky stuff!

Don't stretch the paper when hanging it. It may have a tendency to shrink a bit as it dries.

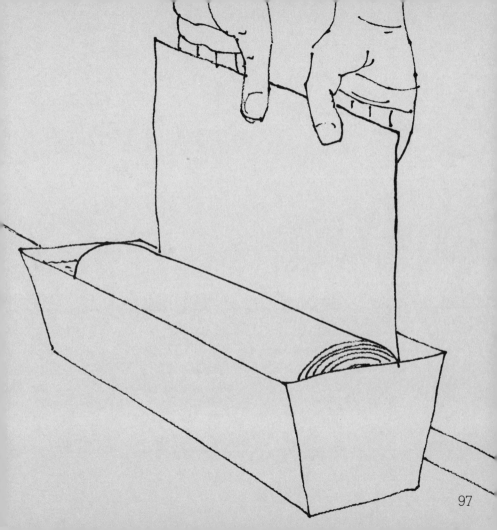

Wall Paneling

You can change the whole personality of a room by paneling one or all the walls with wood, plain or fancy. It's not as hard as it may seem.

If you're working over an existing wall (rather than over bare studs as you would, perhaps, with a room addition or if you were finishing the inside of a garage) the 1/8 inch thick paneling is okay; the 1/4 inch can be easier to work with, and that thickness, or thicker, is a must on bare studs.

Be sure to remove all heat vent, light switch and plug plates and coverings from the wall. You must measure *on* the paneling *exactly* where to cut the openings for such items. Of course, you replace the covers after the paneling is up.

Make certain your first panel goes up *straight*. You can use a plumb bob and line (see "Wallpapering") or use a LEVEL against the side of the panel when you first stick it up.

If you're installing panels on an existing flat wall, you can usually put them up with ADHESIVE (adhesive should reduce, but

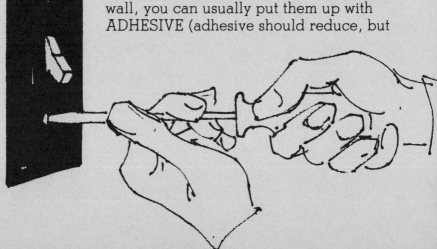

not altogether eliminate the use of nails). The adhesive comes in a tube and works in a caulking gun. Ask where you buy the paneling what adhesive is best for your situation.

Spread adhesive liberally over the wall, one panel at a time. Put the panel in position once, then pull it away from the wall, then set it again. This helps spread the adhesive. Nail panel top and bottom at the vertical joints.

If the wall is irregular or you're installing over concrete or masonry (such as in a basement), you'll need to put up FURRING STRIPS first, to which you nail the panels. Ask at your building supply store for recommendations on your particular needs.

Use a *crosscut* saw to cut panels to fit. Cut with the *good* side of the panel face up. Experts say to measure everything twice! (And cut once!)

Sweep up debris as you go along to avoid tracking dust around the house!

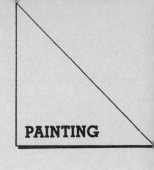

PAINTING

You remember the old line about "painting yourself into a corner"? It's surprisingly easy to do, in one way or another! The biggest problem for amateur painters is not planning ahead! Here are some things to keep in mind before painting almost anything. The person at the paint store should be able to give you plenty of advice, too.

What is the surface to be painted (wood, metal, masonry, etc.)?

What kind of paint is best, latex (water base) or oil base, rubber base, fire-retardant, etc.?

What color paint?

Note: Light colors tend to make a room seem larger. Use of a contrasting color will highlight an area or feature of a room. To conceal features (especially in older places where large vents, radiators or even pipes

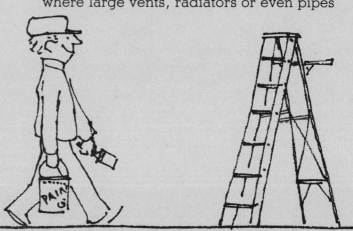

are visible) use the same color as on the walls.

Do you want a glossy or a flat (dull) finish?

What tools will you need besides a brush and probably a roller and pan? Drop cloth or plenty of newspaper to protect floor or furniture, mixing stick, coffee can or plastic bucket, gloves, cap, perhaps a stepladder, something to open paint can lid?

Preparation is as important as the actual painting:

Surface must be clean and dry.

Remove cracked or peeling old paint.

Fill in cracks and holes, be sure filler compound is dry, sand smooth, dust off.

Some people put masking tape around edges or borders where there are contrasting colors or wood. I find this tedious! In any case, you shouldn't put tape over *newly* painted areas (it can peel off the paint when tape is removed).

If you're about to paint a room, remove everything on the walls like switch plates and picture hangers (fill in holes). Protect floor with a drop cloth or newspapers.

Painting a Room

Begin with a brush and paint a 2-3 inch strip around the corners of the room where ceiling joins walls, around door and window frames, above the baseboard. Then, roller the ceiling (unless you skip the ceiling, which I do unless the color won't work or it's just a mess). Next, roller the walls. Now the woodwork, using a brush again and perhaps an enamel paint. Finally, do the baseboard, window frames and door.

Painting Windows

A tedious job! But here's the best way. First, do the sashes (the part that slides up and down). If you have sashes that lift out, you're lucky. In most cases you have to paint 'em in the frame. Raise the bottom sash and lower the top one. Adjust them up and down as you paint, so you can reach all areas, and so that by moving them slightly the paint won't dry sticking to the frame. Moving the sashes once or twice during the drying period should keep them unstuck. Second, paint the pieces (*mullions*) between the glass panes. Some people put masking tape along the edges of the panes to keep paint off. Others keep as steady a hand as possible, then scrape paint off panes after it dries with a razor blade. In any case, use an *angular* sash brush.

The Clean Up

After using water-base paints:

Replace cover on paint can (for any paint). Cover top with an old rag to keep paint from splashing up, then hit it with a hammer.

To clean roller...first, roll out excess paint on newspaper. Remove roller cover, wash in warm soap and water. Rinse several minutes in cool water. Don't squeeze it dry, let it drip dry. Then store in a plastic bag.

To clean brushes... same as for the roller. Hang brushes up, don't leave them sitting in a can of water unless your painting job will take a few days. In that case, keep 'em in water, yes—but don't let them *sit* on the bottom or the bristle will get bent out of shape making your painting chore maddening.

Tape the brush handle to a stick to hold it in the water but off the bottom. In the case of a roller, I've found it lasts well sitting in a little water in the roller pan. Roll out water it's absorbed before using again.

A good way to hang brushes out to dry is on a metal clothes hanger. Cut one edge of the hanger to stick through holes in brush handles. Bend arm of hanger to hold end.

Hang brushes up or lay them flat, covered in plastic or paper, to store them.

If you've used oil or other solvent-thinned paints, you'll need to clean things up with turpentine or some other approved cleaner. Rinse thoroughly in water when finished.

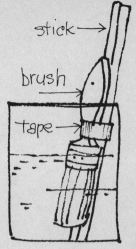

Some Painter's Hints

Use nylon rather than natural bristle brushes with water-base paints.

Use natural bristle with varnish, shellac and enamels, never use nylon!

Before painting raw (new) wood, porous surfaces, patched areas or new wallboard (*drywall*) or plaster, a coat of primer or sealer should be applied. Ask at the paint store what should be put on the specific surface you're dealing with.

Rule of Thumb: Use a roller at least 7 inches wide, little rollers aren't much good; a brush will do an easier, better job in small places.

You can buy an extension rod (in various lengths) that screws into the roller handle and makes it easy to reach upper walls or the ceiling without using a ladder. (Some people swear by it, others think it's too messy!) But remember that painting with a roller inevitably causes some splattering (at least when I use one!) Be aware of the possibility and cover floor or nearby furniture.

Watch where you step! I've kicked over a paint can as well as stepped in spilled paint and tracked it all over the place!

To help minimize small spills and dribbles, tape your can of paint to a square of cardboard or a paper plate (with a loop of masking tape, sticky side out).

Don't paint in a closed-up room, get plenty of fresh air while painting.

Avoid direct inhalation of paint fumes.

To help avoid paint slopping down sides of can after you've dipped the brush in and rubbed off excess against the rim, you can (with hammer and nail) carefully put 5 or 6 holes around the grooved rim so paint can drip back through into can rather than collect in the groove.

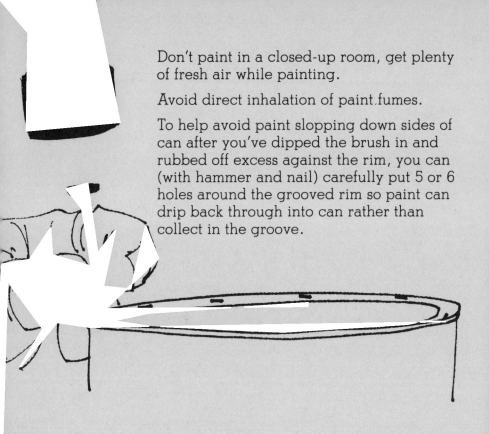

To get loose bristles out of a brush, use an old comb.

Try not to tilt brush *upward* while painting, if you do, paint will run down onto handle (and your hand).

Don't paint with the *side* of a brush.

When using a roller, don't lift it off the surface you're painting during any one application, and don't slide it around—roll it!

Don't smoke or drink alcoholic beverages while using solvent-thinned paints or varnish, etc.

You can paint the baseboard of a room using a PROTECTIVE GUIDE (a plastic one is available at paint stores) or just use a sturdy piece of cardboard held along the floor right next to the baseboard and under each section as you paint it. *Lift* the guide from section to section, don't slide it, to avoid rubbing paint inadvertently along the floor.

When you store leftover paint, don't keep it near a furnace, hot water tank or anywhere near excessive heat or where there are flames. Also, don't leave it outside in a shed where it could freeze in a cold climate.

Aerosol Spray Paint Cans

The nozzle can get clogged, right? If the nozzle is the type that easily pulls off the can, do that and soak it in solvent to try to unclog it. Or, if you have other spray cans with the same kind of nozzle, use one of those nozzles on the can with the clogged one.

To prevent a clogged nozzle: After spraying is complete, invert the can and depress the nozzle. The limited amount of pressure will quickly be exhausted, yet will still blow the nozzle clear of most paint residue and usually prevent clogging.

A popular paint recipe, *often reprinted in almanacs and copied in home manuscript books until well into the nineteenth century,* directed the home owner to *"melt two ounces of Rosin in an iron pot or kettle, add three Gallons of Train Oil and three or four roles of Brimstone: When the Rosin and brimstone are melted and become thin, add as much Spanish Brown, or red or yellow Oker, or any other colour you want as will give the whole as deep a shade as you like, grind them fine, as usual with oil: Then lay it on with a brush as hot and as thin as you can. Some days after the first coat is dried give it a second: It is well attested that this will preserve planck or timber for an age. The work can be done by a common labourer."*

If you have a *Forced Air Furnace*...

Change the filters several times a year, or whenever they become dirty. Dirty filters can even cause the blower motor to keep shutting down (knocking out a circuit breaker or blowing a fuse).

HEATING YOUR HOME

The BLOWER MOTOR and FAN are usually housed behind the furnace firebox. If there's no hot air being blown through your system, the electric motor may be shot. But...check to see that the *fan belt* hasn't broken or slipped off.

117

I've had the motor vibrate loose after years of use, too, which loosened the belt and made the system function poorly. Be sure the MOTOR BRACKETS are secured tightly.

Oil the bearings in the blower fan assembly.

To conserve heat (and energy), wrap the HEAT DUCTS in insulation and be sure all joints in the ducts are sealed (use tape) to keep hot air from escaping (see insulating section).

Vacuum dust and lint out of grates, vents, etc.

On a Gas Burner System...

If nothing works, check that the PILOT LIGHT isn't out. Unless you're really familiar with relighting it, call your utility company or a service person.

On an Oil Burner System...

If things don't work, be sure you're not out of oil! These days that's a distinct possibility!

Also, press the RESET BUTTON on the safety control box, and then try the RESTART BUTTON on the motor.

An oil burning furnace should have a yearly maintenance checkup by a professional.

On a Hot Water Heating System...

Be sure to oil the CIRCULATOR (pump) MOTOR.

Leaky pipes in the system will need a plumber's sure hand, but you can probably deal with the other main problem that arises, air in the system. The radiators or convectors should have air vents (sometimes automatic) which you open with a screwdriver or special key to purge the air from the system. Drops of water will spurt out after all the air has hissed out; close the vent quickly!

If You Have a Steam Heating System...

Be sure each radiator is tilted slightly toward the INLET VALVE (where the pipe carrying the steam joins the radiator). This should alleviate any "radiator hammer"— that banging noise, which I remember as a kid scaring the dickens out of me in the middle of the night!

You may need to adjust the tilt by putting one or more slivers of wood under the radiator, at the opposite end from the inlet valve.

Be sure the AIR VENT on each radiator is *open* and not clogged with dust.

As with any heating system, be sure the THERMOSTAT is working properly and set correctly.

The Fireplace

If smoke comes out of the fireplace rather than going up the chimney . . .

First, put out the fire. Then, ventilate the room when the fire is completely out. Be sure the damper in the flue is open.

Next, relight the fire. Light a twisted newspaper and hold it in the fireplace, this should get the hot air rising. (DO NOT USE ANY PAPER WITH COLORED INKS WHICH CAN RELEASE TOXIC FUMES WHEN BURNED.) Now, relight the kindling or gas starter or logs, etc.

If the problem continues, you probably need to have the chimney cleaned.

Clean the ashes out of the hearth . . . and out of the ashpit before the build-up overwhelms you!

123

Central Air Conditioning

Most systems use the same ductwork and the same blower apparatus that are used for heating.

In any case, oil the blower and replace filters! Note that the CONDENSER AND COMPRESSOR MOTOR UNIT (usually rectangular or round) sits *outside.*

Keep weeds, high grass, bushes, etc. away from this unit, it needs to breathe.

Its filter system needs to be kept clean, too, along with the CONDENSER COILS.

If your unit shuts off due to a power overload, don't try to restart it right away. Air conditioners are tricky, in my experience (which has been mostly bad!), and will start up again when they're good and ready! Continual stopping and starting (or not restarting at all, or kicking out the circuit breaker over and over again) obviously means you've got a problem!

Insulation

To save energy costs and, actually, to be
more comfortable...

Insulate the attic.

Insulate exterior walls, you can even insulate basement walls! Be sure basement windows are tightly shut and preferably sealed with tape or weather stripping of some sort. In my experience (in a humid climate) it's a good idea to keep basement windows sealed in hot weather. This will keep the air conditioning system from sucking in too much warm moisture or condensing it on the cold ducts so that you think it's raining!

Install storm doors and windows...up to 40% of a home's heat loss can be from "leaky" window and door frames.

Put weather stripping around doors and windows, too.

Look around for any holes or cracks that should be patched.

Keep the fireplace damper closed when hearth is not in use, warm air loves to escape up the chimney!

Keep direct sunlight from coming through windows (glass) when you're trying to keep a room cool. Use heavy drapes that can be pulled across large windows or sliding glass doors, especially at night in cold weather or at peak sun periods during hot.

Check out the plastic sheets called INSULATION SHADING—they allow light in through glass, but deflect sun's rays in summer or allow them in during winter.

There are new types of thermostats available which automatically reduce nighttime temperature to cut heating costs.

To get rid of excessive *moisture* in a room or in the basement, try a DEHUMIDIFIER. Be sure the area is closed up—don't leave a basement window open, for example, or moist air will simply keep coming in and the dehumidifier will run forever!

Many people are really intimidated by the outside of their homes—not only the roof and walls and windows, but the shrubs and even the yard. There are a number of things you can do yourself to help preserve the outside of where you live, and save you lots of money in the long run.

Stucco

Cracks in the stucco siding of your house can be easily fixed (and should be, to prevent water or moisture from making them worse or getting at the wood behind the stucco).

Fill *hairline* cracks by just painting over with a thick *masonry* paint.

Larger cracks should be cleaned of loose stucco and dust/dirt; use a hammer and chisel to get out stuck pieces. Use a cold chisel or stonemason's chisel depending upon the depth and width of area to be cleaned. Then, wet the crack and fill it with premixed mortar material (available at hardware or building supply stores). Spread smooth with a putty knife or try to pattern it like the rest of the stucco. Wait three or four days for it to dry thoroughly before painting it to match your house color.

If there's a real hole in your stucco, with building paper and wire or studs showing, get help!

Aluminum Siding

This usually takes no maintenance (you may paint it for looks, not care), but inspect it occasionally to see that it hasn't *warped* at the joints from heat (in which case, get the sections replaced).

Remember that aluminum can *dent*, so don't let kids (or yourself) throw balls against the wall!

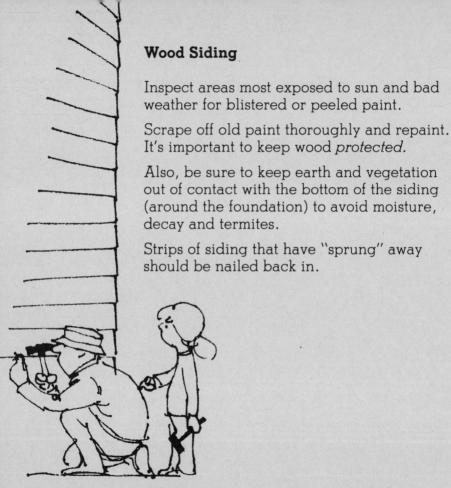

Wood Siding

Inspect areas most exposed to sun and bad weather for blistered or peeled paint.

Scrape off old paint thoroughly and repaint. It's important to keep wood *protected*.

Also, be sure to keep earth and vegetation out of contact with the bottom of the siding (around the foundation) to avoid moisture, decay and termites.

Strips of siding that have "sprung" away should be nailed back in.

Caulking

Caulking means filling in the cracks where two or more sides join. It's essential to keeping the exterior of a house in good shape . . . and keeping water out of the interior!

My first caulking gun provided not only sound weatherproofing but a lot of fun, too! I'd simply never bothered with it before, but once I got going I used up several cartridges (tubes, that is) before I withdrew for the day! A tube of CAULKING COMPOUND fits easily into the metal "gun" frame. Snip off the tip of the plastic nozzle, puncture the inner seal with a nail if necessary, and start squeezing the trigger. When finished, seal the nozzle; put a large nail in it or cover it with masking tape.

Caulking should be applied around all the seams and joints outside the house; such as

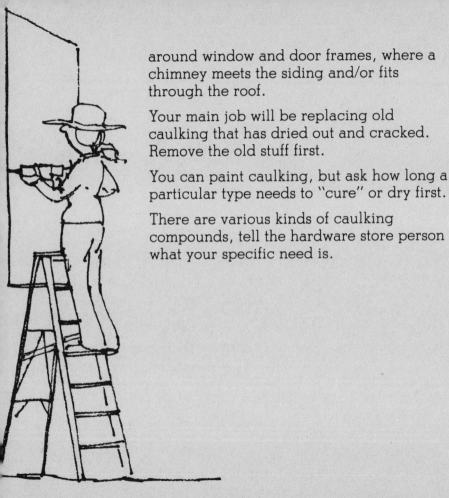

around window and door frames, where a chimney meets the siding and/or fits through the roof.

Your main job will be replacing old caulking that has dried out and cracked. Remove the old stuff first.

You can paint caulking, but ask how long a particular type needs to "cure" or dry first.

There are various kinds of caulking compounds, tell the hardware store person what your specific need is.

Gutters

Keep gutters around the roof clean...
remove leaves, twigs, mud and other junk
that easily collects in them. You can buy a
"clip on" wire mesh that fits over your entire
system to help keep debris out; I've never
used it. It's logical, but looks like a chore to
install!

You could put a screen (or little cage,
available at hardware stores) over the
opening into the downspouts. It's easiest to

136

clean gutters when material collected in them has dried out. You can sweep them clear with a brush or broom.

Trouble is, you can only check to see how well the gutters are working during a pretty hard rain! Sometimes the seams, or joints, of aluminum gutters spring leaks. The guttering channel itself can erode into small holes, too. To repair such leaks, apply ROOFING TAR or ASPHALT ROOF CEMENT (get it in a can at the hardware store). Smear it on with a stick inside the gutter, over the hole or around the seams. Stick a small "patch" of metal over the tar, you can even try using heavy aluminum foil folded a couple of times. Seal over with more tar.

New Screens on Windows and Doors

You can replace worn or broken screens in aluminum frames *yourself!*

First, remove the old screen. Pull out the SPLINES, the thin, rubbery strings that fit down in the CHANNELS that run around the frame and hold in the screen wire.

Remove screen—if it's very old and perhaps rusty, you may have to scrape the stuck bits of wire out of the channels with a putty knife or thin screwdriver.

Now, figure the length and width of new screen you'll need by measuring the *outside* dimensions of the frame.

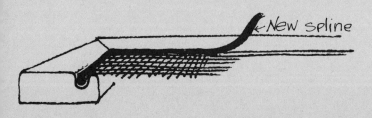

←New spline

Cut the screen to this size.

Line up the screen along adjoining sides of the frame, along the outside edges of the channels, and press or bend screen into the channels. The safest method is to use a SPLINE TOOL available at hardware stores or where you buy the screen. Press screen into all four channels of frame, trim off excess screen.

Next, insert new spline. You can buy this where you got the screen, also. Be sure the spline is the proper size to fit in the channels (doors generally use a larger size than windows). Insert the spline with the tool, and you're done!

Some rather old frames take a very thin spline, by the way, which may not be available. In one such case I used electrical cord instead, the kind that easily separates into two thin strips.

Patching an Asphalt Driveway

A crummy looking driveway does wonders to bring down the appearance of your house! You *can shape it up.*

For small holes, dig out the hole until it's about two inches deep. If the hole is already deeper than that, put small stones and pebbles in to bring it up to the two-inch level.

Buy some ASPHALT PAVER (it comes in bags). Ask at the building supply store how much you'll need, based on the number and size of the holes to be fixed.

Just fill the hole with the paver, tap it in with the flat side of a garden rake, put in more paver and pack it firm. Drive your car over it a few times. Sweep up whatever is left over.

Be sure to work on a warm day, or keep the paver inside at room temperature until you're ready to use it.

For *cracks* in the driveway, use a *sealant*. Mix with some sand to get it real gooey. Spread into the cracks with a trowel. To really add class, give your whole driveway a coat of sealant right out of the can (usually five-gallon cans). This can be a messy job ...wear old clothes and old shoes or boots.

Hose the driveway clean, let it dry.

Pour on sealant a little at a time and spread it smooth with an old broom.

Put up a barricade so no one can turn into the driveway (be sure you didn't leave *your* car in the garage).

It should dry in 24-48 hours, and then it may be slippery for a while.

Power Lawn Mower

If it won't start...

Is there gas in the tank?

Is the stop lever pushed away from the spark plug, (if this is how your machine operates)?

Is the choke-throttle lever working?

Is the spark plug any good?

Note: If you decide to tinker with the engine —be certain not only that it's off, but also remove the spark plug wire so it can't start up accidentally.

For maintenance...

Check oil level before each use (and add if necessary).

Change oil and filter once in a while (when it starts to look all gunky and black).

Clean air cleaner occasionally.

Clean grass off engine, especially around cooling fins and scrape it off blades and from under the housing, especially the area where the grass flies out (or into the grass catcher). BE SURE ENGINE IS OFF AND PLUG WIRE DISCONNECTED BEFORE WORKING *UNDER* THE MOWER!

Have the blade sharpened when you notice "sloppy" cutting.

If the engine stalls out, you may be trying to cut grass that is too high or too wet. Stop mower and see if it's clogged underneath.

Rusty Garden Tools?

Scrub with steel wool, apply rust-remover fluid, scrub again. Now, keep tools in a dry place and clean them off after each use!

GRASS CLIPPER BLADES often seem to get too wide apart so they fold over the grass rather than cutting it! Try tightening the *nut* that controls the "pivot" of the blade that moves, which should tighten the *spring* that holds the blades together.

Garden Hose Woes

When your hose springs a leak, don't throw it away, fix it!

Cut out the leaky, torn, punctured section. Buy a double connector "coupling." Insert it into the two ends of the hose, and be sure the ends are as tight against each other as possible. Then hammer down the prongs on the coupling. If the *nozzle* end is leaking, see if a new washer in the nozzle cures it or else replace the metal piece on the end of the hose with a new "male" coupler.

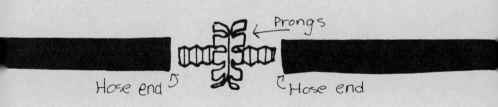

Prongs

Hose end

Hose end

For a leak at the screw (not the faucet) end, put on a new "female" coupler. These come in different diameters, so know your hose size before purchasing.

To cover plants against cold weather, use old panty hose stockings. Peat moss or grass clippings around the base of plants helps, too.

When you water plants or your garden, remember a deep watering is best, not just a sprinkle-over-lightly. The roots go for the water, and should be guided down, not up!

Don't mow newly planted grass until it is at least three inches high.

Give you house a periodic termite inspection. Treat the condition and save a lot of costly repairs later.

The following information should help you maintain your appliances in better running condition, and also help you know what some of their problems are and what to do about them.

First, I must say that most people seem to ignore the instruction booklet that usually comes with a new appliance. My advice: read it cover to cover! Follow the directions for use and care. We need all the help we can get!

When any new equipment is *installed* in your home, try to be there. Ask questions about *use* and *maintenance.* Be sure you know what all the dials and/or switches, etc. really do. Have it tested out before the installers leave.

Keep a record of any appliances you buy: date purchased, from whom, model number, warranty and purchase receipt.

Dishwasher

Personally, I never minded doing dishes by hand. What really turned me on to a dishwasher was the fact it made such a great place to store dirty dishes between washings! At this moment I'm waiting (and have been for weeks) for a part to fix our dishwasher—the soap dispenser! Yes, even that can go ka-put! There's little do-it-yourself fixing on a dishwasher, but here are some things to check if you're having problems.

The door latch must be *completely closed* for the machine to work. See that the LATCH PLATE hasn't gotten lose. Tighten the screws.

Be sure utensils or a dish, or even a piece of a broken dish, haven't jammed the impeller or spray arm (in which case the motor may hum, but there's no action).

If dishes aren't getting clean, the water may not be hot enough. Most experts say 150 degrees is necessary. You can take the machine's temperature with a kitchen or cooking thermometer!

Be sure to use the correct detergent or dishwasher powder for your machine.

If water leaks around the door, see if you find food particles stuck on the door gasket (the rubber seal around the door). Clean gasket carefully. A broken, chipped or worn-out gasket can allow leaks, too.

If dishwasher won't drain, check the hose running into the sink drain. If it looks too tricky to disconnect it, call a service person; if you do disconnect, have a bucket under it to catch water. Of course, if your *sink* drain is clogged, the dishwasher won't drain either.

Hard water, I'm told, will often cause spotting on glassware and silverware. Water that is too soft, or too much detergent, can cause a kind of sanded effect on glassware.

Put silverware in the basket handles facing down and be sure nothing in the basket can slip part way, or all the way through it and interfere with or damage the spray arm. Avoid putting in plastic items that could melt during the drying cycle.

Gas Range

First of all, any time you turn on a burner or oven and it doesn't light within the normal time, TURN IT OFF.

See if the *pilot light* has gone out.

If you smell gas, don't try to relight it. Ventilate the room and call your gas company.

If your pilot lights go out frequently, see if there's a draft of some sort strong enough to blow them out.

An oven door that doesn't fit tightly (food might be stuck on it) can sometimes allow a draft.

Spattering grease can sometimes extinguish a pilot light.

I've also known pilot lights to go out when a burner is turned on! If you notice this, a service person needs to make adjustments.

Be sure you know where the gas turn-off valve is on the line leading into the stove.

If you seem to use the same one or two burners on gas or electric ranges almost all the time, stop! Rotate use of burners so they'll all last longer.

Clean the grease out of the range hood from time to time, and clean the exhaust fan, too.

Refrigerator

This appliance (especially an automatic defrost model) generally just runs and runs and runs. You can keep one running even longer with a little maintenance!

Be sure the machine is *level*.

Don't put it next to the range or any heating unit.

Try to give it some "breathing" room behind and on the sides. Keep it out of the sun, too.

Don't load it with hot food.

Moving the controls to "off" or "defrost" *by mistake* causes trouble more often than you'd imagine!

If the *light* in the fridge doesn't work, the bulb may be burned out or the little pop-in, pop-out button activated by opening and closing the door may have gotten stuck *in*.

A couple of times a year clean the CONDENSER COILS. These are either at the back of the refrigerator or at the base, behind the front panel. Use a vacuum cleaner attachment to clean, but don't dent the coils. Some people put their refrigerator on wheels (rollers, actually) to more easily move it out for cleaning purposes.

Check the gasket around the door. If the motor runs almost continuously, the gasket is probably not doing its job—it's letting cold air out! Stick a piece of paper in around the door, checking it every few inches; if it pulls out *easily* at any point, the gasket is leaking. Get a service person to install a new one.

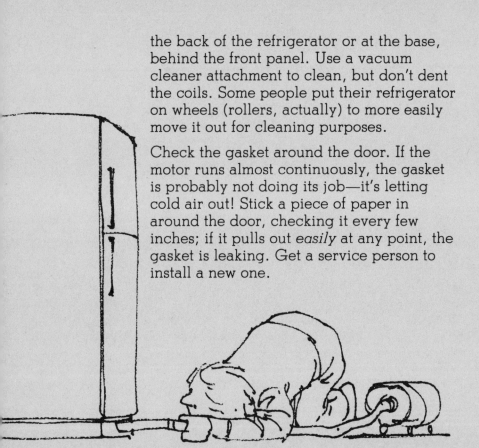

Washing Machine

Turn off water inlets after each use to avoid water pressure build up on hose connections. And be sure to turn them on *before* each use!

Always clean lint trap.

Be sure machine is level.

Don't put in too much soap!

Note: To find out if that appliance repair person who's supposed to see you on a specific day is really coming—call the company first thing that morning and ask for the *dispatcher*. In many cases you'll get one (or someone who handles the chore) and you'll be able to verify that the service call is scheduled. You can usually also find out what number you are on the repair person's route—first, third, eighth, etc. This could give you a better idea of when the person will arrive!

Clothes Dryer

Don't put anything made of plastic or rubber (like baby pants) or anything soaked in cleaning fluid in the dryer. It could cause a mess and/or a fire.

Be sure to clean out lint filter before each use.

Remember, the dryer won't run if the door latch is not completely closed.

Electric dryers have fuses. If your machine isn't running or heating, be sure to check the fuses.

A dryer drum works by a drive belt. Sometimes the belt wears out and breaks. A new one fits easily around the drum and over the motor drive pulley. Remove the front or back panel of the dryer (be sure it's unplugged, of course) to get at the drum. Ask at the appliance store where you buy the new belt for specific instructions for your machine.

Funny noises may mean a bobby pin or
other object is in the drum, or has fallen
part way through a hole and is scraping on
something. Examine the drum.

Vacuum Cleaner

Did you know (or can you imagine) that the first vacuum cleaners, which were made in the early 1900s, weighed as much as sixty pounds! Few appliances take more of a beating. Think about giving your vacuum a break!

Replace or empty the bag before it gets overfull. After about half full, suction will be reduced.

Stop pulling the plug out by the cord!

Quit yanking the machine around and banging it into walls.

Don't vacuum over a still wet (shampooed) carpet, and don't vacuum up solid items such as earrings, bottle caps, hairpins and coins!

On a *canister* or *tank* type, be sure the hose doesn't get clogged. If vacuum isn't whooshing stuff up, remove hose and put your hand over the intake opening. If you feel suction, then it's the hose that must be clogged. Shake it out, or stick a long wire down it. Also, be sure hose is properly attached to canister.

On an *upright* model, the DRIVE BELT sometimes slips off or breaks. It's located right under the machine, a rubber "ring" that hooks the beater brush to the motor shaft.

Turn vacuum upside down, and take off the metal cover. Snap out the brush, slip on belt, replace brush, stretch belt around motor shaft. Also, clean accumulated hair or other material from beater brush. A worn brush should be replaced.

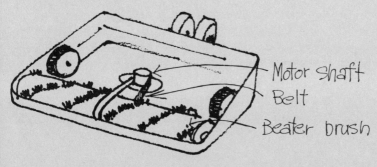

Motor shaft
Belt
Beater brush

Electric Percolator

Of course you know to use *cold* water to start with.

Also, scour out the pot; a dirty one won't perk right.

Be sure cord is plugged in completely. Sometimes a cord may wear out; check that possibility if appliance doesn't work.

Sewing Machine

This is a pretty complex item, at least I think so! Read the instruction booklet for your specific machine; chances are, if you use the machine a lot, you know all about it! However, for the sometime sewer, here are some tips.

Learn about needle-thread tension, use of correct needles (don't use ones that are too long), and the various settings (for example, if the machine is on, but won't sew, see if you forgot to reset the bobbin from "wind").

Also, learn where to *oil* the machine, and how often.

Never try to sew with tangled thread!

Electric Skillet/Grill/Fryer

If you have an older model with *heat controls* built into the appliance rather than removable, *do not* immerse the appliance in water to clean it.

As with any electric appliance, be sure it's plugged in and that current is flowing to the outlet.

Automatic Toaster

Periodically unplug toaster and clean the moving parts on the *hold down* mechanism. Clean the *carriage* tracks inside to remove grease and grime. *Do not* oil tracks or any part of the toaster.

Steam Iron

A little maintenance can go a long way!

If the steam ports (holes) get clogged, put some white vinegar in the iron, heat to steam for a few minutes. Hold the iron horizontally. Unplug iron. Rinse it out carefully. Brush sediment out of the steam holes.

If you seem to get a lot of clogging, your tap water is probably too full of minerals, etc., so use *distilled* water.

Empty water out of iron after each use.

Be sure to set dial exactly, if it's a little off, steam may not work.

Don't overfill with water.

If the iron gets sticky, you can try cleaning it with *very fine* sandpaper. Go over the entire bottom, not just where it's sticky. Then use fine-grain steel wool or a fine soap pad. A solution of baking soda and water may help. Don't nick or scratch the bottom (the sandpaper scratches it a little, but if you go over the whole bottom plate, it evens out).

Garbage Disposal

The main problem you can deal with is a jammed *unit.*

Manually move the IMPELLER (the thing inside with the blades that go round and round). I've used a broom handle or strong stick poked down the machine's mouth and worked counterclockwise.

Some models come with a special *Allen* Wrench that fits into a slot underneath the motor; you just turn the wrench to unjam.

Remember, if disposal doesn't run, push the red *reset* button under the motor—then try the switch again.

Don't drop anything but food into the disposal and read instruction book or ask dealer if there's any food not recommended for the disposal!

Blender

If blender leaks, unscrew metal or plastic bottom, remove blades and gasket, clean thoroughly. If this doesn't work, try a new gasket.

If motor hums, but nothing blends, unplug and carefully see if blades are stuck.

Don't put ice cubes in a blender by themselves, add them one at a time to mixture (to avoid damaging blades).

Electric Knife

If you have a cutting problem, check to be sure food hasn't wedged between the blades. There should be little or no gap between blades, along the scalloped edge. To test gap, run a sheet of ordinary writing paper between the blades; if it runs along easily, with no resistance, blades are too wide apart and should be replaced.

Electric Mixer

If it sparks or smells funny, turn off, unplug. The trouble is in the motor, it could be as simple as worn carbon brushes and springs; but take it to a repair place.

If the motor runs too slowly, you're probably trying to mix too heavy a load!

If you have a bowl and mixer, and the bowl isn't turning, the beaters may be too far from the bottom or there could be something stuck on the bottom of bowl or pedestal. Adjust and/or clean.

Electric Can Opener

Mostly, just keep it clean especially the cutter blade which will get all gunked up with food. The cutter will get dull and must be replaced rather than sharpened. Generally you can just unscrew it and take it with you to buy a new one. Don't lose the little spring that goes with it!

Put a little cooking oil on cutter blade after cleaning.

If the magnet stops holding the cut off lid, take off the magnet and wash it. Get a new magnet if cleaning doesn't work.

If you have a knife sharpener with the can opener, and if you use it a lot, you should clean the metal filings out of the machine periodically. Remove back of appliance and vacuum out filings.

Electric Heater

If you seem to be getting very little heat,
visually check the heating element while it's
on; if you see one or more cool areas while
the rest is glowing, you've got a "short"
which must be repaired. Take it to a fix-it
place!

Battery-Operated Appliances and Games

Periodically check batteries to be sure they haven't worn out and begun to *leak*, which will ruin the item in a hurry. Never store such an item with the batteries in it.

Electric Toothbrush

The works are sealed to make 'em safe to use around water. They're repair proof, so don't try to fix an electric toothbrush that's gone bad. Toss it and buy a new one. Sorry!

Fan

Fans that make annoying vibrations may have a fan blade on the PROPELLER out of alignment. You can replace the whole propeller or try to find the faulty blade and bend it back in line with the others.

Remove propeller and set it face down on a flat surface.

Which blade does not make contact with the surface? This is the culprit. Mark it with chalk. Replace propeller, then bend blade into alignment. Turn on fan; if it still vibrates, turn off and adjust blade further (remember, you might have bent it too much). Continue process until fan runs smoothly.

Room Air Conditioner

Be sure the area immediately outside the window is clear of plants or shrubbery; the unit needs room to breathe.

Clean the FILTER at least once a month. See unit's instruction booklet for best method.

Seal the window around the unit as best you can to keep warm/hot air from entering the room. Keep room closed up generally for best cooling results.

To save energy, if you're gone most of the day attach unit to a timer so it will come on about an hour before you get home.

If unit is in the sun most of the day, some experts say you should put an awning over it.

Oil the fan motor once a year if instructions call for it.

If the COMPRESSOR MOTOR (not the fan) turns on and off repeatedly (called *cycling*), the unit may need cleaning (especially the

CONDENSER COILS), or you may just have to let the unit sit 10 minutes before starting it up again. Also, be sure there's not a window curtain interfering with the cold air flow.

Remember, water normally drips *outside* the unit (from condensation). If water drips inside the window, the unit is probably installed wrong, possibly on an inward tilt or not far enough outside.

CAR CARE

Most of us have had enough nerve-wrenching experiences with car breakdowns and repairs to use up a gross of crying towels! The only advice I can give you is: learn more about your machine.

If you still have the owner's manual, read it! Know where the fuses are, how to get at your spare tire and tools, what all the switches do—things like that.

One way to learn is, when you do get your car serviced, *ask* where items are located. Then you can check a lot of things yourself (probably fix a few), and at least be alert to possible problems and get them looked at before major repairs are necessary. Here is a brief run-down on simplified checkup and maintenance of your car.

Fluids

Your car is always thirsty. Not just for gasoline but other fluids, too.

Oil

Learn where the dipstick is in your car's engine. Check it periodically to see if oil is low or getting dirty. Only check it after the engine has been running, but with engine off.

Use the proper oil (probably a 10W-30 "all-weather" type nowadays) according to your car's maintenance manual. It could make a difference in what basic climate you live, too. Consult a local dealer or service station.

Most experts suggest that you change oil more often than the manual advises if you do most of your driving in the city, for short distances, with lots of stop-start traffic. It is better to change oil more frequently than less.

Change oil filter every-other oil change unless it gets really yucky sooner.

Detergent type oils will appear "dirty" faster than nondetergent oils. This is o.k. because they are removing the "yuck" from the working parts.

Transmission Fluid

This is normally checked during routine "grease 'n oil" change at your service station or dealership. Be sure to *specify* that it's checked!

You can look at *that* dipstick yourself, of course, if you can locate it! Go ahead—ask the service person to show you where it is in your engine next time you get gas!

Engine Coolant and the Radiator

In newer cars, there's a plastic jug (a reserve tank, technically) for the ENGINE COOLANT, it's not called water anymore (in fact, you're better to use a rust inhibitor solution rather than plain water).

You fill the jug rather than the radiator itself; no more dealing with a hot, hissing radiator cap! A small hose connects the reserve tank to the radiator.

You should clean leaves and bugs off your radiator from time to time. Be careful not to dent the core fins or poke a hole in the radiator! You can flush it with a garden hose, under pressure, from inside the engine out through the grill. The CAP on your radiator is, or should be, a pressure cap.

If you have an older car and must add water, coolant or antifreeze, only do so after the engine is off and has been off five minutes or so. Then put a towel or large cloth over the cap and turn counterclockwise very slowly. If steam escapes, wait a moment between turns.

A leaky pressure cap, or a leak in the hoses or connections that carry the engine coolant, will result in an overheated engine. Turn it off at once. Make needed repairs, refill radiator (or reserve tank) before running engine again.

Sometimes a fan belt breaks which causes the water pump and fan not to operate, and your car will overheat in a hurry!

If your temperature gauge shows your car running hot (but not actually boiling over), have the thermostat checked.

Many experts insist you should have your car's cooling system drained (or flushed) every so often—spring and fall, actually! I admit to never having done it—but what do I know?

Antifreeze, obviously, is a *must* in cold climates. Have the freezing point checked by someone competent, be sure it's low enough for the lowest temperature you're likely to get!

Brake Fluid

Yes, brakes work on fluid, too! It's contained in the MASTER CYLINDER under the hood. Once you find it, it's easy to remove the top and check the fluid level if you wish. But . . . if your brakes don't "feel" right . . . or they push all the way to the floor or are very *hard* and hardly push at all . . . or seem to slip or pull to one side or the other—get them checked at once!

Air Cleaner

This is the huge round thing that sits on top of the engine. A nut will unscrew so that you can remove the top of the assembly to change the filter—if you have a "dry element" type. Simply lift it out, shake or carefully tap the gunk out of it, wipe the housing, and replace. Do this every two or three thousand miles. Replace filter when it gets greasy, won't clean out anymore, or gets torn.

There are also "oil bath" and "oil wetted" type filters, which I won't mess with!

Muffler

A lot of noise from under the car probably means the muffler has blown a leak (or your teenager has been messing with it) or else the tailpipe has rusted off its mounting and is dragging on the ground!

Air Conditioner

Get familiar with the SIGHT GLASS under the hood. In normal operation, the glass should be "clear." If you see foam or bubbles in the glass, the system probably needs a change of refrigerant.

It's wise to run your air conditioner once every couple of weeks, even in cold weather, to keep the seals from drying out from disuse.

Tires

Rotate them every five thousand miles.

Radial tires should be rotated on the *same side* of the car only.

If you use snow tires. . . mark them left and right when they're removed, so they get back on correctly next winter.

Keep an eye on tire wear! Abnormal wear ruins a tire and costs you money. Tire wear can be the result of under or over inflation, poor front-end (wheel) alignment, other suspension problems (such as with shock absorbers or springs), and just plain poor driving habits, such as roaring around corners!

Look for cracks or tears in the side walls as well as the tread areas.

Fix a Blinker Signal

Chances are you can replace a burned-out bulb if a service station person won't (and more and more won't these days).

Look inside the trunk, at the back, for tail-light blinkers; and under the hood, behind the grill or even under bumper or fender for front-end blinkers. In any case...the bulb will twist in and out of its metal socket— there are little "knobs" rather than screw threads. Hold the socket when you remove the bulb, otherwise you may pull out a wire. As in all cases when working on your car, be sure the engine *and* ignition are off!

The Clean Car

Everyone knows the person who drives a slum-on-wheels! Well, I'm not out there polishing the hub caps every night. . .but I do believe in a certain amount of wash and wax and paint touch-ups, too (not to mention scooping up the gum wrappers, pebbles, straw, etc. that collect inside).

It only makes sense. . .since this kept-up appearance can mean $$ at trade-in time. Everyone has his or her own peculiar methods of washing and polishing—so I give only a few general hints here.

Soak car first with water, then wash with soap and water. Use a very mild soap (whatever won't give you chapped hands).

Never use anything abrasive. . .if you use an old shirt for a rag, be sure to take off the buttons.

If you live in a winter climate where salt is used on the roads, wash it off as often as possible.

Don't wash or wax in the hot sun.

Do the top first, the wheels last.

If you dry with a cloth, be sure no grit or scratchy dirt gets into it to mar the finish.

Idea: If you have a glass or plastic garden sprayer, put in some dishwashing liquid, fill with water and attach to hose. Now you'll have a sudsy spray!

Finally...frankly, I don't like cars! I was once in a car on a freeway when the vinyl landau roof covering tore free and took on the wind like a sail! The noise sounded like world's end! I have no idea how my maintenance could have prevented this from happening...but it did teach me that your car, no matter how good you are to it, will sooner or later get you!

Index

About the Author

Since childhood when he was growing up in a house built in 1840, Peter Seymour has been coping with fix-it problems. By nature admittedly not a handyman, and seldom in possession of the right tools, Mr. Seymour has had to learn the hard way. Over the years, during a life on the move, he has occupied more than two dozen houses and apartments—each afflicted with the various ailments a home is heir to. No wonder Mr. Seymour has finally learned how to turn a wrench without dislocating his wrist and how to use a hammer without fracturing his thumb. And he feels that if he can do it, you can, too!

About the Designer/Illustrator

Roland Rodegast has repaired, refurbished, puttied, painted, spliced, sanded, fussed, cussed and drawn pictures of it all.

Editorial Direction by Patricia Dreier

Type set in Stymie Light

Printed on Champion Carnival Kraft